*To my daughter and sons*

*Robots are us!*

# Contents

# Acknowledgments

First and foremost, yes! I must extend my deepest gratitude to the brilliant and ever-patient AI language model that has been my steadfast companion throughout this journey of mastering the art of prompt engineering. Had it not been for its tireless ability to generate witty and insightful responses, this book would have been a mere figment of my imagination.

A heartfelt thanks goes out to my family, friends, and colleagues who have been a source of encouragement, laughter, and inspiration during this endeavour. They've endured endless conversations about prompt engineering and have been generous with their own insights and perspectives. Their support has truly been invaluable.

To my fellow beginners in the world of prompt engineering, I hope this book serves as both a guide and a testament to the fact that, with a little determination and a robot by your side, even the most complex of topics can be conquered. While I have certainly learned a lot throughout this process, I must admit that I, too, am still learning. So, should you find any inconsistencies or misguidance within these pages, I kindly ask that you direct your criticisms toward me and not my trusty AI sidekick.

Finally, I would like to express my appreciation to you, dear reader, for embarking on this adventure with me. I trust that this comprehensive guide will inspire you to dive headfirst into the fascinating world of prompt engineering and forge your own path in creating meaningful and engaging conversations with our AI counterparts.

Together, let us embrace this new era of human-AI collaboration, and may our efforts lead to a future where our robotic friends truly understand and delight in the nuanced complexities of human language.

# Acronym

| | |
|---|---|
| AdaIN | Adaptive Instance Normalization |
| AI | Artificial Intelligence |
| ARPANET | Advanced Research Projects Agency Network |
| ATM | Automated Teller Machine |
| BERT | Bidirectional Encoder Representations from Transformers |
| BigGAN | Big Generative Adversarial Network |
| CLIP | Contrastive Language-Image Pretraining |
| COCO | Common Objects in Context (a dataset) |
| DALLE-2 | Deep Abstract Latent Language Exposition 2 |
| EDA | Exploratory Data Analysis |
| FAQs | Frequently Asked Questions |
| GAN | Generative Adversarial Network |
| GPT | Generative Pre-trained Transformer |
| GPT-3 | Generative Pre-trained Transformer 3 |
| GRU | Gated Recurrent Unit |
| IKEA | Ingvar Kamprad Elmtaryd Agunnaryd |
| LSTM | Long Short-Term Memory |
| NLP | Natural Language Processing |
| NLU | Natural Language Understanding |
| RNN | Recurrent Neural Network |
| StyleGAN | Style Generative Adversarial Network |
| TCP | Transmission Control Protocol |
| UNESCO | United Nations Educational, Scientific and Cultural Organization |

VAEs        Variational Autoencoders

XOR         Exclusive OR (a type of logical operation)

# Forward

Prompt engineering is a critical component of natural language processing (NLP) systems, with the potential to transform the way we interact with these systems. As NLP becomes increasingly important in many industries and domains, the need for effective prompt engineering has never been greater. "Mastering Prompt Engineering: A Comprehensive Guide for Beginners" is a practical and comprehensive guide to prompt engineering, providing a detailed introduction to the fundamentals and the latest advances in the field.

This book is written by a team of robots and a novice human learner with little experience in NLP and prompt engineering, just like you I suppose! The team worked together to provide clear and concise explanations of the key concepts and techniques, along with practical examples and case studies to illustrate their applications in real-world scenarios. Whether you are a student, researcher, or practitioner in the field of NLP, this book will at least motivate you or possibly serve as an essential resource for understanding the principles and practices of prompt engineering.

The book is organized into four parts, beginning with an introduction to the fundamentals of prompt engineering and moving on to techniques for effective prompt engineering, applications of prompt engineering, and the future of prompt engineering. Each part is further divided into chapters that provide detailed coverage of the key topics, making the book easy to navigate and understand. I still don't think I should call this a book – rather, sketchy notes. Nevertheless, the document contains the following:

Part 1 provides a comprehensive introduction to the fundamentals of prompt engineering, including its definition, importance, and applications. It also covers the factors affecting prompt engineering, the types of prompts, and the best practices for prompt engineering.

Part 2 covers the techniques for effective prompt engineering, including data collection and preparation, exploratory data analysis, selecting and crafting prompts, and evaluation metrics for prompt engineering. This section also covers the different types of language models and their architectures, along with the common use cases of language models.

Part 3 explores the applications of prompt engineering, including chatbots and virtual assistants, customer service automation, content creation, and fraud detection. Each application is discussed in detail, along with the techniques and strategies used to design and refine prompts for each application.

Finally, part 4 covers the future of prompt engineering, including emerging technologies in AI and machine learning, ethical considerations in prompt engineering, and the challenges and opportunities in the field. This section provides insights into the latest research and developments in prompt engineering, along with practical recommendations for future work and research.

In summary, "Mastering Prompt Engineering: A Comprehensive Guide for Beginners" is an invaluable resource for anyone interested in learning about prompt engineering and its applications in NLP. With its practical and comprehensive approach, this resource is a valuable addition to any NLP library. We, humans and machines, hope that you find this book informative, engaging, and useful in your own work and research. Enjoy!

# NOTE #1

# Introduction

Artificial Intelligence (AI) is a rapidly evolving field that seeks to create intelligent systems capable of performing tasks that typically require human intelligence. This chapter will explore the history, foundational concepts, types, applications, and ethical considerations of AI, providing a comprehensive overview of the field.

**The History of Artificial Intelligence**

The foundations of artificial intelligence (AI) can be traced back to the early 20th century, with the pioneering work of mathematician and logician Alan Turing and his revolutionary concept, the Turing Machine. Turing's ideas laid the groundwork for the development of computer science and the notion that machines could one day perform tasks typically reserved for human intelligence. However, it was not until the 1950s that AI began to emerge as a formal field, marked by the creation of the first computer programs capable of learning and problem-solving.

Over the years, AI research has undergone significant transformation, progressing through various stages of development. Early AI research focused on symbolic reasoning, which involved using logic and symbols to represent and manipulate knowledge. This approach laid the foundation for expert systems in the 1970s and 1980s, which were designed to mimic the decision-making processes of human experts in specific domains.

The current era of AI research has been dominated by the advancements in machine learning and deep learning, which leverage vast amounts of data and sophisticated algorithms to enable machines to learn from experience and improve their performance over time. These cutting-edge techniques have fueled significant breakthroughs in AI capabilities, paving the way for innovations in natural language processing, computer vision, and various other AI applications that continue to reshape our world

## Foundational Concepts

Artificial intelligence (AI) systems are built on a foundation of several key concepts that work together to enable machines to process data, make decisions, and learn from experience. These core concepts include algorithms, machine learning, neural networks, and natural language processing.

### Algorithms

Algorithms are sets of rules and instructions that dictate how an AI system processes data and makes decisions. These algorithms can range from simple, deterministic procedures to complex, probabilistic approaches. They are the backbone of AI systems, guiding their ability to perform tasks and solve problems by transforming input data into meaningful output or actions.

### Machine learning

Machine learning, a subset of AI, is the process through which systems learn from data and improve their performance over time. Machine learning algorithms use statistical techniques to enable computers to adapt and evolve as they are exposed to new data, allowing them to make predictions, recognize patterns, and optimize decision-making processes. Machine learning has been a driving force behind many recent advancements in AI, including image recognition, recommendation systems, and autonomous vehicles.

### Neural networks

Neural networks are computational models inspired by the structure and function of the human brain. They consist of interconnected layers of nodes or neurons that process input data, with each node responsible for performing a specific mathematical operation. Neural networks are particularly effective at recognizing complex patterns and making predictions, which has led to their widespread use in applications such as speech recognition, computer vision, and natural language understanding.

### Natural language processing (NLP)

Natural language processing (NLP) is an area of AI that focuses on enabling machines to understand, interpret, and generate human language. NLP techniques encompass a wide range of tasks, including syntax analysis, semantic understanding, sentiment analysis, and language generation. NLP has made significant strides in recent years, with developments in machine learning and neural networks paving the way for AI systems that can engage in human-like conversation, translate languages, and even generate creative content such as stories and poetry.

## Types of Artificial Intelligence

AI systems can be broadly classified into the following categories:

- Narrow AI: AI systems designed to perform specific tasks, such as image recognition or language translation, without the ability to learn or adapt outside of their domain.

- General AI: Hypothetical AI systems capable of performing any intellectual task that a human can do, possessing the ability to learn and reason across multiple domains.

- Strong AI: AI systems that possess human-like consciousness, self-awareness, and the ability to understand and experience emotions. This type of AI is currently theoretical and remains a topic of debate and speculation.

## Applications of Artificial Intelligence

AI has a wide range of applications across various industries, including:

- Healthcare: AI can be used for diagnosis, treatment planning, drug discovery, and personalized medicine.

- Finance: AI-powered algorithms can detect fraudulent transactions, optimize investment strategies, and improve customer service through chatbots.

- Manufacturing: AI can enhance quality control, optimize supply chains, and enable predictive maintenance.

- Autonomous Vehicles: AI systems can process data from sensors and cameras to enable self-driving cars to navigate and make decisions in real-time.

- Natural Language Processing: AI can be used to develop chatbots, virtual assistants, and language translation tools.

# References

Russell, S. J., & Norvig, P. (2016). Artificial Intelligence: A Modern Approach (3rd ed.). Pearson Education.

Goodfellow, I., Bengio, Y., & Courville, A. (2016). Deep Learning. MIT Press.

Hutter, M., & Auffenberg, K. (2019). An Introduction to Artificial Intelligence. CRC Press.

Turing, A. M. (1950). Computing Machinery and Intelligence. Mind, 59(236), 433-460.

Mitchell, T. M. (1997). Machine Learning. McGraw Hill.

LeCun, Y., Bengio, Y., & Hinton, G. (2015). Deep learning. Nature, 521(7553), 436-444.

Jurafsky, D., & Martin, J. H. (2019). Speech and Language Processing: An Introduction to Natural Language Processing, Computational Linguistics, and Speech Recognition (3rd ed.). Prentice Hall.

Bostrom, N. (2014). Superintelligence: Paths, Dangers, Strategies. Oxford University Press.

Siau, K., & Yang, Y. (2017). Impact of Artificial Intelligence, Robotics, and Machine Learning on Sales and Marketing. In G. G. Preetham (Ed.), AI in Marketing, Sales, and Service (pp. 1-20). Palgrave Macmillan.

Domingos, P. (2015). The Master Algorithm: How the Quest for the Ultimate Learning Machine Will Remake Our World. Basic Books.

Crawford, K., & Whittaker, M. (2016). The AI Now Report: The Social and Economic Implications of Artificial Intelligence Technologies in the Near-Term. AI Now.

Floridi, L., & Cowls, J. (2019). A Unified Framework of Five Principles for AI in Society. Harvard Data Science Review, 1(1).

# NOTE #2

## Natural Language Processing (NLP)

Natural Language Processing (NLP) is a branch of artificial intelligence (AI) that focuses on enabling computers to understand and interpret human language. This technology has been growing rapidly in recent years and has led to many practical applications, such as chatbots, virtual assistants, and automated customer service systems. In this context, a critical component of NLP systems is prompt engineering.

Prompt engineering is the process of designing and refining prompts or input text prompts in a language model to improve the quality and relevance of the generated outputs or responses by the system. Essentially, prompt engineering helps AI systems better understand and respond to human language by crafting the right questions or statements to guide the conversation.

In this book, we will provide an introduction to prompt engineering, exploring its definition, importance, and various applications. Even if you don't have a technical background, this book aims to help you appreciate the significance of prompt engineering and its impact on NLP systems.

### The Importance of Prompt Engineering

Prompt engineering plays a crucial role in the success of NLP systems. Effective prompt engineering can lead to more accurate and relevant responses from the AI, making interactions with chatbots, virtual assistants, or customer service systems feel more natural and helpful. On the other hand, poorly crafted prompts may result in confusing or irrelevant responses, which can lead to user frustration.

Consider the following example: you are interacting with a customer service chatbot, and you ask, "What is the return policy for a purchased item?" An effective prompt might be, "Please provide the order number and date of purchase so that I can look up the specific return policy for your item." This prompt guides the user to provide relevant information that can help the AI system generate an accurate and helpful response. In contrast, a poorly designed prompt might be, "What item are you referring to?" This question does not provide enough context for the user to know what information they should provide, leading to potential confusion and frustration.

Prompt engineering is the process of designing, selecting, and refining prompts or input text for natural language processing (NLP) systems, such as chatbots, virtual assistants, and content generation tools. The primary goal of prompt engineering is to improve the quality, accuracy, and relevance of the responses generated by these systems. By crafting effective prompts, developers can guide the AI system to provide more contextually appropriate, meaningful, and useful outputs based on user input or a specific task. In essence, prompt engineering is a critical step in optimizing the performance of NLP systems and ensuring meaningful interactions between humans and AI.

**Definition of Prompt Engineering**

Prompt engineering involves selecting or crafting prompts that will elicit the desired type of response from the NLP system. The prompt is the input text provided to the system, which it uses to generate the output or response. A well-designed prompt should be informative and clear, providing the necessary context for the system to generate an accurate and relevant response.

Prompt engineering involves analyzing the system's strengths and weaknesses to create prompts that leverage its strengths and address its weaknesses. This analysis includes understanding the characteristics of the task or problem the system is being used for and tailoring the prompts to fit those characteristics. The process also involves selecting the appropriate data to train the model and evaluating the effectiveness of the prompts.

Prompt engineering is a key part of creating systems that use language processing, which are tools that help computers understand and interact with humans using our language. Think of it as teaching a computer to speak human - and sometimes even understand our jokes! Examples of these systems include chatbots, virtual assistants like Amazon's Alexa, and tools that create content like articles or product descriptions. Prompt engineering is all about designing the right questions or statements (called prompts) to get the best possible answers or responses from the computer system, so it doesn't sound like a robot impersonating Shakespeare.

# NOTE #3

**Why Prompt Engineering Matters**

Prompt engineering is essential because the quality of the prompts determines the quality of the responses. If a prompt is unclear or poorly designed, the computer system might give inaccurate or unhelpful answers - or worse, it could start reciting bad knock-knock jokes. Here are some examples of why prompt engineering is important:

(a) **CHATBOTS**

Chatbots, also known as conversational agents or virtual assistants, have become an increasingly popular tool for businesses, organizations, and individuals to streamline communication and provide efficient customer service. These AI-powered programs simulate human conversation through text or voice interactions, enabling users to ask questions, request information, or perform tasks without direct human intervention.

**History and Development**

The concept of chatbots dates back to the 1960s, with the creation of ELIZA, an early natural language processing program developed by Joseph Weizenbaum. ELIZA mimicked human conversation by recognizing keywords in user inputs and generating scripted responses. Over the years, the development of chatbots has evolved, with advancements in artificial intelligence, machine learning, and natural language processing, leading to more sophisticated conversational agents.

**Types of Chatbots**

There are two primary types of chatbots: rule-based and AI-based. Rule-based chatbots rely on predefined rules and decision trees to respond to user queries, which means they can only handle specific scenarios and may struggle with complex or ambiguous inputs. In contrast, AI-based chatbots use natural language processing, machine learning, and sometimes even deep learning techniques to understand user inputs, learn from interactions, and generate more accurate and contextually relevant responses.

**Applications and Use Cases**

Chatbots have a wide range of applications across various industries, including but not limited to:

- Customer Service: Chatbots are commonly used for customer support, providing instant responses to frequently asked questions, troubleshooting issues, and guiding users through processes such as placing orders or booking appointments.

- E-commerce: In the e-commerce sector, chatbots can assist customers with product recommendations, provide information on shipping and returns, and even facilitate the checkout process.

- Healthcare: Chatbots can serve as virtual health assistants, providing users with symptom assessments, appointment scheduling, medication reminders, and general health information.

- Finance: Financial institutions use chatbots to offer services such as account balance inquiries, transaction tracking, bill payments, and investment advice.

- Human Resources: Chatbots can streamline HR processes by answering employee questions about policies, benefits, and procedures, as well as assisting with tasks like leave requests and performance evaluations.

- Education: Educational institutions and e-learning platforms utilize chatbots to provide personalized learning experiences, answer questions about courses, and offer study tips or resources.

## Challenges and Limitations

Despite their numerous benefits, chatbots also face several challenges and limitations. Some of these include:

- Understanding context and ambiguity: Chatbots can struggle with understanding the context of a conversation or dealing with ambiguous inputs, which may lead to incorrect or irrelevant responses.

- Language limitations: Most chatbots are designed to understand and communicate in specific languages, which might limit their use in multilingual environments.

- Lack of empathy and emotional intelligence: Chatbots are not capable of truly understanding human emotions, which can result in responses that may seem insensitive or inappropriate in certain situations.

## (b) VIRTUAL ASSISTANTS

Virtual assistants, also known as digital assistants or voice assistants, are AI-powered applications designed to help users perform tasks and access information through natural language voice commands. These intelligent systems have become an integral part of modern life, offering assistance in various aspects of our daily routines, from managing schedules to controlling smart home devices.

## History and Development

The rise of virtual assistants can be traced back to the 1990s, with the introduction of Apple's voice recognition software, PlainTalk. However, it wasn't until 2011 that the concept of virtual assistants gained widespread popularity with the launch of Apple's Siri. Since then, other tech giants, including Amazon, Google, and Microsoft, have developed their own virtual assistants, such as Alexa, Google Assistant, and Cortana, respectively. These systems have evolved significantly over time, thanks to advancements in artificial intelligence, machine learning, and natural language processing.

## Types of Virtual Assistants

Virtual assistants can be categorized into two main types: personal and enterprise. Personal virtual assistants, such as Siri, Alexa, and Google Assistant, are designed for individual users and are commonly found on smartphones, smart speakers, and other consumer electronics. These assistants help users with tasks like setting reminders, playing music, and answering general questions.

Enterprise virtual assistants, on the other hand, are tailored for businesses and organizations. These assistants can perform more specialized tasks, such as managing customer support inquiries, scheduling meetings, or handling sales queries.

## Applications and Use Cases

Virtual assistants have a broad range of applications, some of which include:

- Personal Productivity: Virtual assistants can help users manage their schedules, set reminders, send messages, make phone calls, and provide directions.

- Home Automation: By integrating with smart home devices, virtual assistants can control lights, thermostats, security systems, and other appliances through voice commands.

- Entertainment: Virtual assistants can play music, read audiobooks, and provide recommendations for movies, TV shows, and games.

- Travel and Hospitality: Virtual assistants can assist users in booking flights, hotels, and car rentals, as well as provide recommendations for local attractions and restaurants.

- Customer Service: Businesses can use virtual assistants to provide 24/7 support, answering frequently asked questions and handling customer complaints or inquiries.

- Accessibility: Virtual assistants can offer valuable assistance to individuals with disabilities or impairments, helping them access information and perform tasks more easily.

**Challenges and Limitations**

While virtual assistants have made significant strides in recent years, they still face several challenges and limitations:

- Language and Accent Recognition: Virtual assistants can struggle with understanding different languages, dialects, and accents, which can lead to misunderstandings and frustration for users.

- Contextual Understanding: Virtual assistants can have difficulty understanding the context or nuances of certain requests, resulting in incorrect or unhelpful responses.

- Privacy Concerns: The use of virtual assistants raises concerns about user privacy, as these systems often require access to personal information and have the potential to store sensitive data.

## (c) CONTENT CREATION

Content creation is the process of producing and sharing valuable, relevant, and engaging information in various formats, such as articles, videos, images, podcasts, and social media posts. The primary goal of content creation is to attract, inform, entertain, and retain an audience, ultimately leading to increased brand awareness, customer loyalty, and business growth. With the rapid evolution of digital technologies and the growing importance of online presence, content creation has become a vital aspect of modern marketing strategies.

**The Content Creation Process**

The content creation process typically involves several key steps:

- Identifying the target audience: Understanding the interests, needs, and preferences of the intended audience is crucial for creating content that resonates with them.

- Setting clear objectives: Defining the goals of the content, such as generating leads, increasing website traffic, or boosting brand awareness, helps guide the creation process and measure success.

- Brainstorming ideas: Generating a list of potential topics and content formats that align with the target audience's interests and the established objectives.

- Conducting research: Gathering relevant data, insights, and resources to create well-informed and accurate content.

- Crafting the content: Producing the content using engaging storytelling techniques, compelling visuals, and clear, concise language.

- Editing and refining: Ensuring the content is polished and free of errors, while also optimizing it for search engines and user experience.

- Distributing and promoting: Sharing the content through various channels, such as social media, email marketing, and content syndication platforms, to reach the target audience and maximize exposure.

- Analysing performance: Using analytics tools to track the content's performance and making data-driven adjustments to improve future content creation efforts.

## The Role of AI in Content Creation

Artificial intelligence (AI) has begun to play a significant role in content creation, with advancements in natural language processing (NLP) and machine learning algorithms enabling the development of AI-powered tools that can generate written content, design graphics, and even produce videos. These tools can help streamline the content creation process, reduce workload, and enhance the quality of the output. However, it is essential to use AI responsibly and maintain a balance between automation and human creativity to ensure that the content remains engaging, unique, and relevant to the target audience.

## Types of Content Formats

Content creation can take many forms, and it is essential to choose the right format for the intended audience and objectives. Some popular content formats include:

- Blog posts and articles: Written content that covers various topics, often used to inform, educate, or entertain readers.

- Videos: Engaging and visually appealing content that can be used for product demonstrations, tutorials, or storytelling.

- Infographics: Visually striking representations of data, facts, or complex concepts that make it easy for the audience to understand and retain the information.

- Podcasts: Audio content that covers various topics and can be consumed on-the-go, offering an alternative to written or visual content.

- Social media posts: Short-form content shared on social media platforms, designed to spark engagement and conversation.

- eBooks and whitepapers: In-depth, long-form content that explores a specific topic, often used as a lead generation tool.


**Examples of Prompt Engineering**


There are many ways prompt engineering is used to create helpful language processing systems. Here are some examples:

**Automatic Summarization:** This is when a computer system creates a shorter version of a longer text. Prompt engineering helps the system understand what parts of the text are most important for the summary - so it doesn't just spit out a summary that says, "Once upon a time... The End."

**Sentiment Analysis:** This is a way to figure out the emotions expressed in a piece of text. Prompt engineering helps the system understand the specific emotion being discussed - because no one wants a computer telling them they're angry when they're just feeling a bit hangry.

**Language Translation:** Prompt engineering is important for systems that translate text from one language to another, ensuring that the translations are accurate and make sense - and not like something you'd find on a poorly translated menu in a foreign country.

**Automated Question Answering:** Some computer systems are designed to answer questions people ask. Prompt engineering helps these systems understand the question and provide a useful answer - and not just reply with "Because I said so."

**Fraud Detection:** In finance, prompt engineering can be used to create systems that spot unusual or suspicious activity, helping to prevent fraud - and not just flag every transaction involving a suspiciously large number of rubber ducks.

## Conclusion

Prompt engineering is an important part of creating systems that use language processing. These systems need well-designed prompts to provide accurate and useful responses to users. Prompt engineering is used in many different ways, from chatbots and virtual assistants to content creation and fraud detection.

To create effective prompts, it's important to understand the strengths and weaknesses of the computer system, the specific task it's being used for, and how to evaluate whether the prompts are working well. By focusing on prompt engineering, we can make sure language processing systems are more accurate and useful in a wide range of applications - and maybe even get a few laughs along the way.

So, when you think of prompt engineering, remember that it's not just about making computers speak our language - it's about making them speak it with style, grace, and sometimes even a sense of humor. After all, who wouldn't want a chatbot that can not only answer their questions but also share a funny joke or two?

By embracing prompt engineering, we can help ensure that language processing systems not only understand our requests but also respond in a way that's engaging, informative, and, when appropriate, downright entertaining. The future of communication with AI lies in the delicate balance between utility and wit, and prompt engineering is the key to unlocking that delightful combination.

# References

Allen, G., & Chan, T. (2019). Artificial Intelligence and Content Creation. In G. G. Preetham (Ed.), AI in Marketing, Sales, and Service (pp. 95-110). Palgrave Macmillan.

Brownlee, J. (2017). Deep Learning for Natural Language Processing. Machine Learning Mastery.

Carey, J. (2015). Content Strategy: Connecting the Dots Between Business, Brand, and Benefits. XML Press

Gartner, Inc. (n.d.). Chatbots in Customer Service. Retrieved from https://www.gartner.com/en/information-technology/insights/chatbots

Goldberg, Y. (2017). Neural Network Methods for Natural Language Processing. Morgan & Claypool Publishers.

Hirschberg, J., & Manning, C. D. (2015). Advances in natural language processing. Science, 349(6245), 261-266.

Hutto, C. J., & Gilbert, E. (2014). VADER: A Parsimonious Rule-based Model for Sentiment Analysis of Social Media Text. In Proceedings of the Eighth International Conference on Weblogs and Social Media (ICWSM).

Jurafsky, D., & Martin, J. H. (2019). Speech and language processing: An introduction to natural language processing, computational linguistics, and speech recognition (3rd ed.). Prentice Hall.

Kumar, A., Gupta, K., & Varma, V. (2020). Prompting Systems in NLP: A Review. arXiv preprint arXiv:2012.15765.

Manning, C. D., & Schütze, H. (1999). Foundations of Statistical Natural Language Processing. MIT Press.

McTear, M., Callejas, Z., & Griol, D. (2016). The Conversational Interface: Talking to Smart Devices. Springer.

Shawar, B. A., & Atwell, E. (2007). Chatbots: Are they really useful? LDV Forum, 22(1), 29-49.

Shevat, A. (2017). Designing Bots: Creating Conversational Experiences. O'Reilly Media.

Vaswani, A., Shazeer, N., Parmar, N., Uszkoreit, J., Jones, L., Gomez, A. N., ... & Polosukhin, I. (2017). Attention is All You Need. In Advances in Neural Information Processing Systems (NIPS).

# NOTE #4

# Understanding Language Models

Once upon a time in the world of computers, understanding and generating human language was a challenging task. But then came the language models, making it easier for computers to comprehend and create human-like text. So, what is a language model? It's like a wizard that helps computers understand the magic of human language. Let's dive deeper into the enchanting realm of language models and see how they make our lives more exciting and convenient.

Imagine you're playing a game of "fill in the blanks" with a friend, and you have to guess the next word in a sentence. A language model does something similar, but it's a mathematical wizard that uses its knowledge of the language to predict what word comes next. By learning from a treasure trove of text called a corpus, the language model becomes a master of the language's patterns and rules.

Language models play a starring role in many fascinating applications that make our lives easier. From magically translating text into different languages to listening and understanding our voices, they have the power to change how we interact with technology.

Now, let's explore some of the different types of language models that help bring the magic of human language to life.

# Introduction to Language Models

Welcome to the fascinating world of language models, where computers learn to understand and generate human-like text. Language models are a core component of natural language processing (NLP), which is a subfield of artificial intelligence (AI) that focuses on enabling machines to read, understand, and generate text in a way that mimics human language.

## I. Types of Language Models

### N-GRAM MODELS

These are the simplest types of language models. N-gram models are based on the frequency of word sequences (n-grams) in a corpus of text. An n-gram is a contiguous sequence of n items (usually words) from a given sample of text. For example, in a bigram model (2-gram), the probability of a word is estimated based on its preceding word. N-gram models are computationally efficient and relatively easy to implement. However, they come with several limitations, such as their inability to capture long-range dependencies between words and their reliance on fixed context sizes.

Applications of n-gram models
N-gram models are suitable for low-resource environments due to their computational efficiency. They are often used for tasks such as text classification, spelling correction, and simple language generation. N-gram models can also serve as a baseline for more complex language models or be combined with other techniques to improve performance.

Challenges and drawbacks
N-gram models have several limitations. They have an inability to capture long-range dependencies between words, as the context size is fixed to n-1 words. This can lead to poor performance on tasks that require understanding of longer phrases or sentences. Additionally, n-gram models are sensitive to data sparsity issues, as they rely on the frequency of word sequences in the training data. This can result in poor generalization to new, unseen text.

NEURAL NETWORK-BASED MODELS

These are more advanced models that use deep learning techniques to learn language patterns from large datasets. Neural network-based language models leverage the power of artificial neural networks to identify complex relationships between words and their context. These models are capable of capturing longer-range dependencies and understanding the underlying structure of a language. Some common types of neural network-based models include recurrent neural networks (RNNs), long short-term memory (LSTM) networks, gated recurrent units (GRUs), and transformers. These models have significantly improved the state of the art in NLP tasks such as machine translation, sentiment analysis, and text summarization. However, they can be computationally intensive and require larger amounts of data for training compared to n-gram models.

I. Recurrent Neural Networks (RNNs)

RNNs are a type of neural network that can process sequential data. They are particularly useful for language modeling because they can capture long-range dependencies between words. However, RNNs suffer from the vanishing gradient problem, which can make it difficult for them to learn long-term dependencies. This issue arises when gradients during backpropagation become very small, causing the weights in the network to stop updating effectively.

II. Long Short-Term Memory (LSTM) Networks

LSTM networks are a type of RNN that can solve the vanishing gradient problem by introducing memory cells that can store information over time. These memory cells allow LSTMs to learn and remember long-range dependencies between words. LSTMs have been used extensively in various NLP tasks, including machine translation, text summarization, and sentiment analysis.

III. Gated Recurrent Units (GRUs)

GRUs are another type of RNN that are similar to LSTMs but have fewer parameters. They use gating mechanisms to control the flow of information in the network, allowing them to capture long-range dependencies between words while being more computationally efficient than LSTMs. GRUs have been used in a variety of NLP tasks, such as language modeling, machine translation, and speech recognition.

# NOTE #5

## Transformers and Advanced Language Model Architectures

### I. Transformers

Transformers are a relatively new type of neural network architecture introduced by Vaswani et al. in 2017. They use self-attention mechanisms to weigh the importance of each word in a sequence relative to other words in the sequence, allowing them to capture complex dependencies and relationships between words. Transformers have become a dominant force in natural language processing due to their ability to handle long-range dependencies and parallelize computation, making them highly efficient and scalable.

Transformers are particularly useful for generating long-form text and understanding context in natural language processing tasks. They have been successfully applied to a wide range of tasks, including machine translation, text summarization, sentiment analysis, question answering, and language modeling. Their ability to handle large-scale, high-dimensional data has made them the go-to architecture for many state-of-the-art NLP models.

### II. Popular Transformer-Based Models

A. BERT (Bidirectional Encoder Representations from Transformers): BERT is a powerful transformer-based model developed by researchers at Google AI Language. It understands context and relationships between words by pre-training on a large corpus of text and fine-tuning for specific tasks. BERT's bidirectional training allows it to learn deep contextualized word embeddings, which can be fine-tuned to achieve state-of-the-art performance on a wide range of NLP tasks, such as named entity recognition, sentiment analysis, and question answering.

B. GPT (Generative Pre-trained Transformer): GPT is a large-scale language model developed by OpenAI that leverages the transformer architecture. It is designed for advanced text generation and question-answering tasks, among others. GPT is pre-trained on a massive corpus of text and can be fine-tuned for specific tasks. The most recent version, GPT-3, (hold on , I know we now have GPT- 4) has generated significant interest due to its ability to generate high-quality, human-like text and perform a wide array of tasks with minimal fine-tuning, making it a versatile and powerful tool in natural language processing.

## III. Future Directions

*Advancements in language model architectures:*

As computational power and access to data continue to grow, we can expect further advancements in language model architectures. Researchers are constantly exploring new techniques and algorithms to improve the efficiency, accuracy, and scalability of language models. These advancements will likely lead to the development of even more powerful models capable of handling increasingly complex tasks, further pushing the boundaries of natural language processing. Additionally, emerging trends, such as multi-modal models that combine text, images, and other types of data, will expand the capabilities of language models and enable new applications across various domains.

*Ethical considerations in language model development*

As language models become more powerful and ubiquitous, it is essential to address the ethical considerations surrounding their development and use. This includes ensuring fairness and reducing biases in model training data, which can inadvertently perpetuate harmful stereotypes or discriminatory behavior. Moreover, the potential for misuse of advanced language models, such as generating misleading or harmful content, should be addressed through responsible development practices and the establishment of ethical guidelines. The research community, industry stakeholders, and policymakers must collaborate to create a framework that balances innovation with social responsibility.

Language models play a crucial role in improving human-computer interaction by enabling more natural, intuitive, and efficient communication between humans and machines. As these models continue to evolve, we can expect a greater degree of personalization and context-awareness in technologies such as virtual assistants, chatbots, and customer support systems. This will allow for more seamless integration of technology into our daily lives and open up new opportunities for enhancing productivity, collaboration, and accessibility. In conclusion, the ongoing advancements in language model architectures will continue to transform the field of natural language processing, with far-reaching implications for the ways we interact with technology and the world around us.

## Common Use Cases of Language Models

Language models have numerous practical applications in NLP systems. The following are some common use cases of language models:

- Machine Translation: Machine translation is the process of translating text from one language to another. Language models can be used to generate translations by predicting the probability of a sequence of words in the target language given a sequence of words in the source language.

- Speech Recognition: Speech recognition is the process of converting spoken language into text. Language models can be used to improve speech recognition accuracy by predicting the most likely sequence of words given an audio input.

- Chatbots and Virtual Assistants: Chatbots and virtual assistants rely on language models to generate responses to user queries. The language model analyzes the user's input and generates a response that is relevant and coherent.

- Text Generation: Language models can be used to generate text, such as product descriptions, news articles, and social media posts. These models can generate text that is coherent and grammatically correct, making them useful for content creation.

- Sentiment Analysis: Sentiment analysis is the process of identifying the sentiment or emotion expressed in a piece of text. Language models can be trained to predict the sentiment of a given piece of text, which can be useful for sentiment analysis applications such as social media monitoring.

- Automatic Summarization: Automatic summarization is the process of creating a condensed version of a longer piece of text. Language models can be used to generate summaries by predicting the most important sentences or phrases in the text.

- Language Modeling: Language modeling is the process of predicting the probability of a sequence of words in a language. Language models can be used to improve the accuracy of other NLP tasks by providing a measure of the likelihood of a given sequence of words.

- Spell and Grammar Checking: Language models can be employed to enhance spell and grammar checking tools by predicting the most probable word sequence or suggesting corrections based on context.

- Autocomplete and Predictive Text: Language models can suggest words or phrases to users as they type, improving typing efficiency and accuracy by predicting the most likely next word based on context.

- Named Entity Recognition: Language models can help identify and classify named entities such as people, organizations, and locations within text, enabling more effective information extraction.

- Question Answering Systems: Language models can be used to develop systems that provide answers to specific questions, extracting relevant information from large datasets or knowledge bases.

- Paraphrase Generation: Language models can generate paraphrases of given text, enabling tasks like data augmentation, text simplification, and plagiarism detection.

- Text Classification: Language models can be employed to classify text into categories, such as topic detection or spam filtering.

- Code Completion: Language models can be trained on programming languages to offer code suggestions or autocomplete features, increasing developer productivity.

- Natural Language Interface: Language models can be used to create interfaces that allow users to interact with software using natural language, making the software more accessible and user-friendly.

- Medical Text Analysis: Language models can help analyze medical text data like electronic health records and research articles to extract valuable insights and improve healthcare outcomes.

- Legal Document Analysis: Language models can assist in analyzing legal documents for compliance, risk assessment, or contract review.

- Customer Support Automation: Language models can be used to automate customer support by providing instant, accurate answers to user questions and reducing response times.

- Content Filtering and Moderation: Language models can detect and filter inappropriate or offensive content in social media platforms or online forums.

- Personalized Content Recommendations: Language models can analyze user preferences and behavior to provide personalized content recommendations, improving user engagement and satisfaction.


## Negative Use Cases of Language Models

Language models, while offering numerous beneficial applications, can also be exploited for harmful purposes. These include generating deepfakes to spread misinformation, fostering online harassment and cyberbullying, producing convincing spam and scams, and propagating disinformation and fake news. Additionally, they can be utilized to manipulate public sentiment, promote radicalization and recruitment, impersonate real individuals, enable automated plagiarism, contribute to biased decision-making, and invade personal privacy. As the power of language models continues to grow, it is crucial to remain vigilant and develop safeguards against their potential negative consequences.

- Deepfake Generation: Language models can generate highly realistic deepfake text, audio, or video content that can be used to spread misinformation, manipulate public opinion, or cause harm to individuals' reputations.

- Online Harassment and Cyberbullying: Malicious actors can use language models to automate the generation of offensive, threatening, or abusive messages targeting individuals or groups, exacerbating online harassment and cyberbullying.

- Automated Spam and Scams: Language models can be employed to create convincing spam emails or phishing messages, tricking users into revealing sensitive information or downloading malicious software.

- Disinformation and Fake News: Language models can generate false news articles or disinformation campaigns, undermining trust in media and contributing to the spread of false information.

- Manipulation of Public Sentiment: Language models can be used to manipulate public sentiment by generating targeted propaganda or misleading narratives on social media platforms, influencing public opinion on sensitive topics.

- Radicalization and Recruitment: Language models can generate extremist content or propaganda, contributing to the radicalization and recruitment of vulnerable individuals to extremist ideologies or organizations.

- Impersonation: Language models can be used to impersonate real individuals, creating fake social media profiles or emails that can be used for fraud, identity theft, or other malicious purposes.

- Automated Plagiarism: Language models can generate high-quality, original-looking content based on existing sources, enabling large-scale plagiarism that can undermine the integrity of academic and professional work.

- Biased Decision-Making: If language models are trained on biased datasets, they may perpetuate or even exacerbate existing biases in their output, leading to unfair or harmful consequences in applications such as hiring, lending, or medical diagnosis.

- Privacy Invasion: Language models can potentially be used to analyse and infer sensitive information from seemingly innocuous text data, such as social media posts, potentially violating individuals' privacy and leading to unintended consequences.

## Conclusion

Language models are a critical component of NLP systems that can generate and understand human language. There are two main types of language models: n-gram models and neural network-based models. Neural network-based models are becoming increasingly popular due to their ability to capture complex relationships between words.

The architecture of a language model refers to the structure of the neural network that is used to generate or understand text. Common language model architectures include RNNs, LSTMs, GRUs, and transformers.

Language models have numerous practical applications in NLP systems, including machine translation, speech recognition, chatbots and virtual assistants, text generation, sentiment analysis, automatic summarization, and language modeling. Understanding language models is critical to developing effective NLP systems that can generate and understand human language.

# References

Bengio, Y., Ducharme, R., Vincent, P., & Jauvin, C. (2003). A neural probabilistic language model. Journal of Machine Learning Research, 3(Feb), 1137-1155.

Chen, X., Liu, Y., & Liu, Z. (2020). Neural language models: Architectures, training, and applications. ACM Transactions on Intelligent Systems and Technology (TIST), 11(1), 1-36.

Cho, K., Van Merriënboer, B., Gulcehre, C., Bahdanau, D., Bougares, F., Schwenk, H., & Bengio, Y. (2014). Learning phrase representations using RNN encoder-decoder for statistical machine translation. arXiv preprint arXiv:1406.1078.

Devlin, J., Chang, M. W., Lee, K., & Toutanova, K. (2018). BERT: Pre-training of deep bidirectional transformers for language understanding. arXiv preprint arXiv:1810.04805.

Goldberg, Y. (2016). A primer on neural network models for natural language processing. Journal of Artificial Intelligence Research, 57, 345-420.

Hirschberg, J., & Manning, C. D. (2015). Advances in natural language processing. Science, 349(6245), 261-266.

Hochreiter, S., & Schmidhuber, J. (1997). Long short-term memory. Neural computation, 9(8), 1735-1780.

Jurafsky, D., & Martin, J. H. (2019). Speech and language processing: An introduction to natural language processing, computational linguistics, and speech recognition (3rd ed.). Prentice Hall.

LeCun, Y., Bengio, Y., & Hinton, G. (2015). Deep learning. Nature, 521(7553), 436-444.

Mikolov, T., Chen, K., Corrado, G., & Dean, J. (2013). Efficient estimation of word representations in vector space. arXiv preprint arXiv:1301.3781.

Radford, A., Narasimhan, K., Salimans, T., & Sutskever, I. (2018). Improving language understanding by generative pre-training.

Sutskever, I., Vinyals, O., & Le, Q. V. (2014). Sequence to sequence learning with neural networks. In Advances in neural information processing systems (pp. 3104-3112).

Vaswani, A., Shazeer, N., Parmar, N., Uszkoreit, J., Jones, L., Gomez, A. N., ... & Polosukhin, I. (2017). Attention is all you need. In Advances in neural information processing systems (pp. 5998-6008).

Vaswani, A., Shazeer, N., Parmar, N., Uszkoreit, J., Jones, L., Gomez, A. N., ... & Polosukhin, I. (2017). Attention is all you need. Advances in Neural Information Processing Systems, 30, 5998-6008.

# NOTE #6

# Fundamentals of Prompt Engineering

Prompt engineering is a critical component of natural language processing (NLP) systems that involves designing and refining prompts or input text prompts in a language model. The goal of prompt engineering is to improve the quality and relevance of the generated outputs or responses by the system. In this chapter we (human and machine) are going to provide an in-depth discussion of the fundamentals of prompt engineering, including how it works, factors affecting prompt engineering, types of prompts, and best practices for prompt engineering.

I know you are now happy we are going to start the prompting finally!

**How Prompt Engineering Works**

Prompt engineering involves selecting or crafting prompts that will elicit the desired type of response from the NLP system. The prompt is the input text provided to the system, which it uses to generate the output or response. A well-designed prompt should be informative and clear, providing the necessary context for the system to generate an accurate and relevant response.

The process of prompt engineering involves analysing the system's strengths and weaknesses to create prompts that leverage its strengths and address its weaknesses. This analysis includes understanding the characteristics of the task or problem the system is being used for and tailoring the prompts to fit those characteristics. The process also involves selecting the appropriate data to train the model and evaluating the effectiveness of the prompts.

**Definition of "prompt"**

In the context of prompt engineering, a "prompt" refers to the input given to a language model to guide its response or output. Prompt engineering is the process of designing and refining these input queries to effectively communicate the desired task to the language model and obtain more accurate, relevant, and useful results.

A well-crafted prompt helps the model understand the context and intention of the request, making it more likely to generate appropriate and high-quality responses. Prompt engineering may involve testing various phrasings, adding context, or providing examples to guide the model's understanding of the desired output. This process is particularly important when working with large-scale language models, such as OpenAI's GPT models, to optimize their performance in a wide range of tasks and applications.

## Key Elements of a Prompt

A prompt is a starting point or an instruction that guides an AI language model to generate a specific response or output. The key elements of an effective prompt are:

- Clarity: The prompt should be clear and concise, providing enough information for the language model to understand the desired output. Avoid ambiguity and use specific wording to reduce the chances of misinterpretation.

- Context: Providing context in a prompt helps the language model generate more relevant and accurate responses. This may involve giving background information or explaining the purpose of the task.

- Instruction: Clearly state the task or question that the language model needs to address. Make sure the instruction is precise and easy to understand.

- Constraints: If the response needs to follow specific guidelines or limitations, such as a word count or format, include those constraints in the prompt.

- Examples (optional): Including examples in the prompt can help guide the language model towards the desired output. This can be particularly useful when asking for a specific type of response or when the task is complex.

- Gradual Information Reveal (optional): In some cases, breaking down the prompt into smaller pieces and feeding the information gradually can help the model better understand the task and generate more accurate responses.

- Tone and Style: Consider the tone and style of the desired output. Adjust the prompt accordingly to encourage the language model to generate responses that match the desired tone, whether it's formal, informal, persuasive, or informative.

**Factors Affecting Prompt Engineering**

Several factors can affect prompt engineering, including the following:

- Task or Problem: The task or problem the system is being used for will affect the type of prompts that should be used. For example, a chatbot designed for customer service will require different prompts than a language model designed for language translation.

- Data Quality: The quality of the data used to train the model will affect the effectiveness of the prompts. High-quality data that is relevant to the task or problem will result in better prompts and better performance from the system.

- Domain Expertise: Domain expertise is essential in prompt engineering. Experts in the domain can provide insights into the characteristics of the task or problem, which can inform the selection and crafting of prompts.

- Evaluation Metrics: Evaluation metrics are used to measure the effectiveness of the prompts. The choice of evaluation metrics will affect the type of prompts that are used and the overall performance of the system.

**Types of Prompts**

Prompt engineering is an essential aspect of designing effective interactions with AI language models. There are various types of prompts that can be used, depending on the desired outcome, as follows:

- Closed Prompts: Closed prompts are prompts that require a specific response from the system, such as a yes/no answer or a multiple-choice question. Closed prompts are useful for tasks that require a specific type of response.

- Open Prompts: Open prompts are prompts that allow for a wide range of responses from the system. Open prompts are useful for tasks that require the system to generate creative or diverse responses.

- Structured Prompts: Structured prompts are prompts that provide a specific format for the response. Structured prompts are useful for tasks that require a specific structure or format for the response, such as filling out a form.

- Unstructured Prompts: Unstructured prompts are prompts that do not provide a specific format for the response. Unstructured prompts are useful for tasks that require the system to generate free-form responses.

## Importance of AI prompt engineering and prompting

AI prompt engineering and prompting are important for several reasons:

- Enhanced Language Understanding: Prompt engineering helps AI systems to better understand and process human language by providing well-designed inputs that guide the model towards more accurate and relevant responses. This leads to improved natural language understanding and better performance in various language processing tasks.

- Context-aware Responses: By crafting effective prompts, AI systems can better comprehend the context of a request, leading to more appropriate and meaningful responses. This makes AI-based applications, such as chatbots and virtual assistants, more user-friendly and valuable.

- Tailored Solutions: Prompt engineering allows developers to customize AI systems for specific tasks and applications, ensuring that the generated output meets the unique requirements of the use case. This customization makes AI tools more versatile and suitable for a wide range of industries and scenarios.

- Efficiency and Time Savings: Effective prompting can help AI systems provide faster and more accurate responses, reducing the time and effort required for users to find information or complete tasks. This can lead to increased productivity and efficiency in both personal and professional settings.

- Improved User Experience: When AI systems generate relevant and engaging responses, users are more likely to have a positive experience with the technology. Prompt engineering plays a critical role in ensuring that AI systems deliver value and satisfaction to users, ultimately fostering trust and widespread adoption of AI-based solutions.

- Evaluation and Optimization: Prompt engineering also involves the evaluation of AI system performance and making adjustments to improve the effectiveness of the prompts. This iterative process helps developers fine-tune AI models, ensuring they continually improve and adapt to new challenges and requirements.

**Best Practices for Prompt Engineering**

- Effective prompt engineering requires careful consideration and attention to detail. The following are some best practices for prompt engineering:

- Data Collection and Preparation: High-quality data that is relevant to the task or problem is essential for effective prompt engineering. The data should be cleaned, pre-processed, and formatted to ensure that it is suitable for training the model.

- Exploratory Data Analysis (EDA): EDA involves analysing the data to understand its characteristics, such as the distribution of words and the frequency of different types of text. EDA can help inform the selection and crafting of prompts.

- Selecting and Crafting Prompts: Prompts should be selected or crafted to fit the characteristics of the task or problem. The prompts should be informative and clear, providing the necessary context for the system to generate an accurate and relevant response.

- Evaluating Prompts: Evaluating the effectiveness of the prompts is critical to prompt engineering. The choice of evaluation metrics should be relevant to the task or problem, and the evaluation should be conducted on a diverse set of data to ensure that the prompts generalize well.

- Iterative Design: Prompt engineering is an iterative process that involves refining the prompts based on feedback from the evaluation. The prompts should be updated and refined based on the results of the evaluation until the desired level of performance is achieved.

- Domain Expertise: Domain expertise is essential in prompt engineering. Experts in the domain can provide insights into the characteristics of the task or problem, which can inform the selection and crafting of prompts.

# References

Brown, T. B., Mann, B., Ryder, N., Subbiah, M., Kaplan, J., Dhariwal, P., Neelakantan, A., Shyam, P., Sastry, G., Askell, A., Agarwal, S., Herbert-Voss, A., Krueger, G., Henighan, T., Child, R., Ramesh, A., Ziegler, D. M., Wu, J., Winter, C., ... Amodei, D. (2020). Language Models are Few-Shot Learners. arXiv preprint arXiv:2005.14165.

Brownlee, J. (2020). How to Develop a Deep Learning Model to Generate Text for a Chatbot with Keras. Retrieved from https://machinelearningmastery.com/how-to-develop-a-deep-learning-model-to-generate-text-for-a-chatbot-with-keras/

Devlin, J., Chang, M. W., Lee, K., & Toutanova, K. (2018). BERT: Pre-training of deep bidirectional transformers for language understanding. arXiv preprint arXiv:1810.04805.

Dodge, J., & Gane, A. (2019). Fine-tuning Language Models from Human Preferences. Retrieved from https://arxiv.org/pdf/1909.08593.pdf

GPT-3: Language Models are Few-Shot Learners. (2020). Retrieved from https://openai.com/blog/language- models-are-few-shot-learners/

Lample, G., & Conneau, A. (2019). Cross-lingual Language Model Pretraining. Retrieved from https://arxiv.org/pdf/1901.07291.pdf

Manning, C. D., & Schütze, H. (1999). Foundations of Statistical Natural Language Processing. MIT Press.

Radford, A., & Salimans, T. (2021). DALL·E: Creating Images from Text. Retrieved from https://openai.com/blog/dall-e/

Radford, A., Narasimhan, K., Salimans, T., & Sutskever, I. (2018). Improving Language Understanding by Generative Pre-Training.

Sharma, P., Shukla, S., & Gupta, A. (2021). Evaluating NLP Models: A Comprehensive Guide. Retrieved from https://towardsdatascience.com/evaluating-nlp-models-a-comprehensive-guide-f5a5a2800bce

Vaswani, A., Shazeer, N., Parmar, N., Uszkoreit, J., Jones, L., Gomez, A. N., Kaiser, Ł., & Polosukhin, I. (2017). Attention is all you need. In Advances in Neural Information Processing Systems (pp. 5998-6008).

# NOTE #7

## Techniques for Effective Prompt Engineering

Prompt engineering is the process of designing and refining prompts to improve the quality and relevance of the generated responses from natural language processing (NLP) systems. Effective prompt engineering is critical to the success of NLP systems, as the prompts play a crucial role in shaping the responses generated by the system. In this book, we discuss some techniques for effective prompt engineering, including data collection and preparation, exploratory data analysis (EDA), selecting and crafting prompts, and evaluation metrics for prompt engineering.

### Data Collection and Preparation

Effective prompt engineering requires high-quality data that is relevant to the task or problem at hand. The data should be collected and prepared carefully to ensure that it is suitable for training the NLP system. The following are some best practices for data collection and preparation:

Define the Data Requirements: The first step in data collection and preparation is to define the data requirements based on the characteristics of the task or problem at hand. This involves determining the type of text, the language, and the domain of the text.

Identify and Collect the Data: Once the data requirements have been defined, the next step is to identify and collect the data. The data should be diverse and representative of the task or problem at hand.

Clean and Preprocess the Data: The data should be cleaned and preprocessed to remove any irrelevant or redundant information. This involves removing stop words, punctuation, and special characters, as well as performing other preprocessing steps, such as stemming and lemmatization.

Format the Data: The data should be formatted in a way that is suitable for training the NLP system. This involves converting the data into a format that can be used by the NLP system, such as tokenization or encoding.

**Exploratory Data Analysis (EDA)**

EDA is a critical step in prompt engineering that involves analyzing the data to gain insights into its characteristics. EDA can help inform the selection and crafting of prompts and can also help identify potential issues with the data. The following are some best practices for EDA:

Identify the Characteristics of the Data: The first step in EDA is to identify the characteristics of the data, such as the distribution of words and the frequency of different types of text.

Visualize the Data: Data visualization can help identify patterns and trends in the data that may not be apparent from numerical summaries. Common visualization techniques include histograms, word clouds, and scatter plots.

Identify Potential Issues with the Data: EDA can help identify potential issues with the data, such as missing data or outliers. These issues should be addressed before the data is used to train the NLP system.

# Selecting and Crafting Prompts

Selecting and crafting prompts is a critical component of prompt engineering that involves designing prompts that elicit the desired type of response from the NLP system. The following are some best practices for selecting and crafting prompts:

**Understand the Task or Problem**

The prompts should be designed based on an understanding of the task or problem at hand. This involves analyzing the strengths and weaknesses of the NLP system and tailoring the prompts to fit those characteristics.

**Consider the User**

The prompts should be designed with the user in mind. They should be informative and clear, providing the necessary context for the NLP system to generate an accurate and relevant response.

**Leverage Domain Expertise**

Domain expertise is essential in prompt engineering. Experts in the domain can provide insights into the characteristics of the task or problem, which can inform the selection and crafting of prompts.

**Consider the Type of Prompt**

Different types of prompts may be more suitable for different tasks or problems. Closed prompts may be more suitable for tasks that require a specific type of response, while open prompts may be more suitable for tasks that require the NLP system to generate creative or diverse responses.

**Use Existing Data**

Existing data can be used to generate prompts, such as using frequently asked questions or user reviews to generate prompts for a chatbot or virtual assistant.

# Evaluation Metrics for Prompt Engineering

**Evaluation Metrics for Prompt Engineering**

Assessing the effectiveness of prompts in generating accurate and relevant responses is crucial for successful prompt engineering. The choice of evaluation metrics significantly impacts the types of prompts used and the overall performance of the NLP system. Some common evaluation metrics for prompt engineering include:

**Accuracy**

Accuracy is a widely used metric to measure the effectiveness of prompts. It calculates the percentage of correct responses generated by the NLP system in comparison to the total number of responses.

**Precision and Recall**

Precision and recall are essential metrics for evaluating the effectiveness of prompts in tasks such as information retrieval or classification. Precision measures the percentage of relevant responses generated by the NLP system, while recall measures the percentage of relevant responses that were successfully retrieved.

## F1 Score

The F1 score combines precision and recall into a single metric, providing a balanced measure of the two values. It is especially useful when both precision and recall are equally important for the task at hand.

## Perplexity

Perplexity is a metric employed to evaluate the effectiveness of language models. It measures the degree of uncertainty in the model's predictions, with lower perplexity scores indicating better performance. Lower perplexity means that the model is less "perplexed" or confused by the text it is processing.

## Human Evaluation

Human evaluation involves enlisting human evaluators to rate the quality of responses generated by the NLP system. This approach provides insights into the effectiveness of the prompts that may not be captured by other metrics, as human evaluators can consider factors such as coherence, relevance, and creativity. Human evaluation is particularly valuable when dealing with open-ended or creative tasks, where objective metrics may not adequately capture the nuances of the generated responses.

The choice of evaluation metrics should be tailored to the specific requirements of the task and the desired outcomes. A combination of these metrics can provide a comprehensive understanding of the effectiveness of prompts, ultimately leading to better performance in NLP systems.

## Conclusion

Prompt engineering is a critical component of NLP systems that involves designing and refining prompts to improve the quality and relevance of the generated responses. Effective prompt engineering requires careful consideration and attention to detail, including data collection and preparation, EDA, selecting and crafting prompts, and evaluation metrics for prompt engineering. With careful planning and execution, prompt engineering can help improve the accuracy and relevance of NLP systems, which can have a wide range of practical applications.

## References

Cai, Y., Liu, S., Zhang, Y., & Wen, W. (2019). Prompt Tuning for Few-Shot Learning. Retrieved from https://arxiv.org/pdf/2007.04898.pdf

Chen, X., Liu, Y., & Liu, Z. (2020). Neural language models: Architectures, training, and applications. ACM Transactions on Intelligent Systems and Technology (TIST), 11(1), 1-36.

Liu, S., Cai, Y., Zhang, Y., & Wen, W. (2020). A Simple Framework for Contrastive Learning of Visual Representations with Few-Shot Classification. Retrieved from https://arxiv.org/pdf/2012.07177.pdf

Wang, H., Chen, M., & Hovy, E. (2021). Learning to Generate Questions by Learning to Create Questions. Retrieved from https://arxiv.org/pdf/2101.09406.pdf

Yuan, Y., & Huang, J. (2020). Prompt-based Transfer Learning for Zero-Shot and Few-Shot Text Classification. Retrieved from https://arxiv.org/pdf/2012.15715.pdf

# NOTE #8

## Selecting and Crafting Prompts

Prompt engineering is the art of designing and refining prompts to enhance the quality and relevance of responses generated by natural language processing (NLP) systems. The success of NLP systems heavily relies on effective prompt engineering, as prompts play a crucial role in guiding the system to produce appropriate responses. This article delves into some applications of prompt engineering, including chatbots and virtual assistants, customer service automation, content creation, and fraud detection.

**Chatbots and Virtual Assistants**

Chatbots and virtual assistants represent some of the most prevalent applications of prompt engineering. The success of these AI-driven conversational agents depends significantly on prompt engineering, as it shapes the dialog between the user and the system. Here are a few examples illustrating the use of prompt engineering in chatbots and virtual assistants:

- Designing User Flows: User flows consist of sequences of prompts that navigate the conversation between the user and the chatbot or virtual assistant. To develop effective user flows, one must carefully plan and execute the selection and crafting of prompts, ensuring they provide sufficient context for the system to generate accurate and relevant responses.

- Natural Language Understanding (NLU): NLU entails processing the user's input, comprehending its meaning, and producing contextually appropriate responses. To achieve effective NLU, prompt engineering must involve the creation of carefully designed prompts that offer the necessary context for the system to accurately interpret the user's input and generate suitable responses.

- Multilingual Support: Providing multilingual support in chatbots and virtual assistants is heavily dependent on effective prompt engineering. This support necessitates the development of well-crafted prompts that cater to the user's specific language and cultural background, ensuring that the system remains relevant and effective across various linguistic contexts.

## Customer Service Automation

Prompt engineering is also used in customer service automation, where chatbots and virtual assistants are used to automate customer service tasks. The following are some examples of how prompt engineering is used in customer service automation:

- Frequently Asked Questions (FAQs): FAQs are a common application of prompt engineering in customer service automation. Effective FAQs require carefully crafted prompts that provide the necessary information to answer common customer questions.

- Customer Complaints: Prompt engineering is used to guide the conversation between the customer and the system to resolve customer complaints. Effective prompt engineering can help improve customer satisfaction by providing accurate and relevant responses to customer complaints.

- Escalation: Prompt engineering can be used to identify when a customer's problem requires escalation to a human agent. Effective prompt engineering can help identify when escalation is necessary and provide the necessary information to the human agent to resolve the problem.

## Content Creation

Prompt engineering is also used in content creation, where NLP systems are used to generate content such as news articles, social media posts, and product descriptions. The following are some examples of how prompt engineering is used in content creation:

- News Articles: Prompt engineering can be used to generate news articles based on a specific topic or event. Effective prompt engineering can help generate accurate and relevant news articles that provide the necessary context for the reader.

- Social Media Posts: Prompt engineering is used to generate social media posts that are appropriate for the platform and the target audience. Effective prompt engineering can help generate engaging and informative social media posts that generate engagement from the target audience.

- Product Descriptions: Prompt engineering can be used to generate product descriptions that accurately describe the product's features and benefits. Effective prompt engineering can help generate product descriptions that are informative and persuasive.

**Fraud Detection**

Prompt engineering is also used in fraud detection, where NLP systems are used to detect fraudulent activity such as phishing and identity theft. The following are some examples of how prompt engineering is used in fraud detection:

- Phishing Detection: Prompt engineering can be used to detect phishing attempts by analyzing the language used in the prompts. Effective prompt engineering can help identify phishing attempts and prevent users from falling victim to them.

- Identity Theft Detection: Prompt engineering can be used to detect identity theft by analyzing the language used in the prompts. Effective prompt engineering can help identify attempts to steal personal information and prevent users from becoming victims of identity theft.

- Fraudulent Transactions: Prompt engineering can be used to detect fraudulent transactions by analyzing the language used in the prompts. Effective prompt engineering can help identify transactions that are suspicious or fraudulent and prevent users from becoming victims of fraud.

**Conclusion**

Prompt engineering is a critical component of NLP systems that has a wide range of practical applications, including chatbots and virtual assistants, customer service automation, content creation, and fraud detection. Effective prompt engineering requires careful consideration and attention to detail, including data collection and preparation, EDA, selecting and crafting prompts, and evaluation metrics for prompt engineering. With careful planning and execution, prompt engineering can help improve the accuracy and relevance of NLP systems, which can have a significant impact on many industries and domains.

# References

Deng, L., & Yu, D. (2014). Deep learning: methods and applications. Foundations and Trends® in Signal Processing, 7(3–4), 197-387.

Gao, H., & Huang, S. (2021). Intelligent Customer Service System Based on NLP Technology. In Proceedings of the 2021 International Conference on Artificial Intelligence and Computer Science (pp. 15-19).

Hao, Y., & Li, W. (2019). A Brief Survey of Prompt Engineering for Open-Domain Dialogue Systems. arXiv preprint arXiv:1910.10434.

Kurdi, M. F., & Farghaly, M. S. (2021). Applications of Natural Language Processing Techniques in Customer Service. In Proceedings of the 2021 International Conference on Computer and Information Sciences (pp. 55-60).

Mensah, S., & Baiden, E. A. (2020). Machine Learning and Deep Learning Techniques for Fraud Detection: A Comprehensive Review. International Journal of Intelligent Systems and Applications in Engineering, 8(4), 67-80.

# NOTE #9

## *Future of Prompt Engineering*

Prompt engineering is a rapidly evolving field that has the potential to transform the way we interact with natural language processing (NLP) systems. With advances in machine learning and artificial intelligence (AI), prompt engineering is becoming more sophisticated and capable of generating more accurate and relevant responses. In this book, we discuss the future of prompt engineering, including emerging technologies, ethical considerations, and challenges and opportunities.

### Emerging Technologies in Prompt Engineering

The future of prompt engineering is closely tied to emerging technologies in AI and machine learning. The following are some emerging technologies that are likely to have a significant impact on prompt engineering:

- Generative Pre-trained Transformer 3 (GPT-3): GPT-3 is a powerful language model developed by OpenAI that is capable of generating human-like text. GPT-3 has the potential to revolutionize prompt engineering by enabling more accurate and relevant responses to be generated.

- Few-Shot Learning: Few-shot learning is a machine learning technique that enables NLP systems to learn from a small amount of data. Few-shot learning has the potential to reduce the amount of data required for prompt engineering and enable more rapid development of NLP systems.

- Reinforcement Learning: Reinforcement learning is a machine learning technique that involves training an agent to interact with an environment to achieve a goal. Reinforcement learning has the potential to enable NLP systems to learn from feedback and improve over time.

# NOTE #10

## Ethical Considerations in Prompt Engineering

As prompt engineering evolves and becomes more complex, it is crucial to address the ethical implications associated with its use. This section will explore some of the key ethical considerations in prompt engineering, including bias, privacy, and transparency, as well as strategies to mitigate potential ethical concerns.

### Bias

Bias in prompt engineering may occur if the data used to train the NLP system contains biased information. This can lead to unfair or discriminatory outcomes, such as the generation of biased responses towards certain groups of people. To address bias in prompt engineering, consider the following steps:

- Diverse and Representative Data: Ensure that the data used for training the NLP system is diverse and representative of various demographics and perspectives, reducing the risk of biased outcomes.

- Regular Auditing: Continuously monitor and audit the performance of the NLP system to identify and rectify any unintended biases in the generated responses.

- Bias Mitigation Techniques: Implement bias mitigation techniques, such as re-sampling, re-weighting, or adversarial training, to reduce the impact of bias on the NLP system's outputs.

### Privacy

Privacy concerns may arise in prompt engineering if the NLP system is used to collect, store, or process personal information. To protect user privacy and ensure the ethical use of data, consider the following steps:

- Data Anonymization: Anonymize any personal data collected from users to protect their identities and ensure compliance with data protection regulations.

- Data Usage Policies: Develop clear and transparent data usage policies, informing users about the collection, processing, and storage of their data, as well as their rights regarding their personal information.

- Secure Data Storage and Processing: Implement strong data security measures to protect users' personal data from unauthorized access, tampering, or loss.

## Transparency

Transparency concerns may emerge in prompt engineering if the NLP system does not clearly disclose how it generates responses. To enhance transparency and promote user trust, consider the following steps:

- Explainable AI: Develop explainable AI systems that provide users with insights into the decision-making process of the NLP system, making it easier for users to understand how the system generates responses.

- Clear Documentation: Provide comprehensive and accessible documentation on the NLP system's functionality and underlying algorithms, enabling users to better comprehend the system's workings.

- User Control: Offer users control over the NLP system's behavior, such as adjusting the system's settings or providing feedback on generated responses, to foster a sense of trust and transparency.

## Challenges and Opportunities in Prompt Engineering

- Prompt engineering faces several challenges and opportunities as it continues to evolve. The following are some challenges and opportunities in prompt engineering:

- Data Quality: The quality of data used to train NLP systems can have a significant impact on the accuracy and relevance of the generated responses. It is important to ensure that data is high-quality and representative of the task or problem at hand.

- Multimodal Input: Prompt engineering is currently focused on text-based input, but there is increasing interest in multimodal input, such as speech and images. Prompt engineering will need to evolve to support multimodal input and generate responses that are appropriate to the input.

- Human-in-the-Loop: Human-in-the-loop is an approach that involves having humans provide feedback to the NLP system to improve its performance. Human-in-the-loop can help improve the accuracy and relevance of the generated responses and enable the NLP system to learn from feedback.

# References

Brown, T. B., Mann, B., Ryder, N., Subbiah, M., Kaplan, J., Dhariwal, P., ... & Amodei, D. (2020). Language models are few-shot learners. arXiv preprint arXiv:2005.14165.

Hao, Y., & Li, W. (2019). A Brief Survey of Prompt Engineering for Open-Domain Dialogue Systems. arXiv preprint arXiv:1910.10434.

Joshi, M., Peters, M. E., Hopkins, M., Goyal, N., & Uszkoreit, J. (2020). Beyond English-only QA: Cross-lingual Few-shot Question Answering with Unsupervised Machine Translation. arXiv preprint arXiv:2004.09813.

Krizhevsky, A., Sutskever, I., & Hinton, G. E. (2012). ImageNet classification with deep convolutional neural networks. In Advances in neural information processing systems (pp. 1097-1105).

Liu, Y., Ott, M., Goyal, N., Du, J., Joshi, M., Chen, D., ... & Stoyanov, V. (2020). Roberta: A robustly optimized bert pretraining approach. arXiv preprint arXiv:1907.11692.

Nogueira, R., & Cho, K. (2019). Passage re-ranking with bert. arXiv preprint arXiv:1901.04085.

# NOTE #11

## Layout of Prompts

Creating a layout for a prompt involves organizing the components and structure of the prompt to guide an NLP system effectively. Here's a layout that can be used to design your prompts:

*Context*

a. Background: Provide the necessary background information or context to set the stage for the prompt.

b. Constraints: Define any limitations or constraints that apply to the response.

*Task Definition*

a. Objective: Clearly state the goal or objective of the task the NLP system needs to accomplish.

b. Requirements: Specify any requirements, such as format, length, or structure, for the response.

*Examples (optional)*

a. Sample Input: Provide an example of a typical input, if necessary, to help the NLP system understand the format and structure of the input.

b. Sample Output: Provide an example of a typical output, if necessary, to help the NLP system understand the desired format and structure of the response.

# Prompting techniques

Prompting techniques are crucial for effective communication with AI language models like ChatGPT. They help guide the AI model to provide more accurate, relevant, and context-specific responses. Here are some common types of prompting techniques and the differences between them:

Simple prompts: These are basic, single-word or short-phrase prompts that provide minimal guidance to the AI model. Simple prompts can generate a wide variety of responses, but they may not be as precise or contextually relevant as more specific prompts.

Elaborate prompts: These prompts provide more detailed information and context, allowing the AI model to generate more accurate and relevant responses. Elaborate prompts can include multiple sentences, specific requirements, or even questions to guide the AI model's response.

Step-by-step prompts: These prompts break down a task or question into smaller, sequential steps to guide the AI model in providing a more structured and detailed response. Step-by-step prompts are especially useful when asking the AI model to describe a process or provide a set of instructions.

In-the-style-of prompts: These prompts instruct the AI model to generate responses in a specific style, tone, or format. For example, the prompt could ask the AI model to write a response in the style of a particular author, mimic a specific genre, or use a specific writing technique.

Negation and affirmation prompts: These prompts explicitly instruct the AI model to either include or exclude specific elements in the response. Negation prompts can help eliminate undesired content, while affirmation prompts emphasize the inclusion of specific details or requirements.

Iterative prompts: These prompts involve refining and re-submitting the original prompt based on the AI model's previous response. Iterative prompting can help improve the quality and relevance of the AI model's output by providing additional context or clarification.

Conversational prompts: Conversational prompts engage the AI model in a back-and-forth dialogue to elicit more information or to clarify specific points. These prompts can be particularly useful for extracting information from the AI model and refining its understanding of the user's intent.

Each prompting technique has its strengths and weaknesses, and the choice of technique depends on the specific task, desired output, and context. In practice, users may combine multiple prompting techniques to achieve the best results when interacting with AI language models.

# NOTE #12

# Example of Prompts for Generative Pre-trained Transformer (GPT)

**Below are examples of prompts for ChatGPT**

ChatGPT is a language model developed by OpenAI, based on the GPT (Generative Pre-trained Transformer) architecture. It is designed to understand and generate human-like text, making it suitable for a wide range of natural language processing tasks. ChatGPT can be used in various applications, such as chatbots, virtual assistants, content generation, question-answering, and more. As an AI model, ChatGPT is trained on large datasets of text from the internet to learn patterns, context, and language structure. It uses the transformer architecture, which allows it to effectively capture long-range dependencies and context within the text. When given a prompt, ChatGPT generates coherent, relevant, and contextually appropriate responses based on its understanding of the input and its training data.

## Example 1: Health

*Context*
a. Background: The user wants to know about the health benefits of drinking green tea.
b. Constraints: The response should be concise and focused on health benefits only.
Task Definition
a. Objective: List the health benefits of green tea.
b. Requirements: Provide a bullet-point list of at least five health benefits.
*Examples (optional)*
a. Sample Input: "What are the health benefits of drinking green tea?"
b. Sample Output:
Improves brain function
Increases fat burning
Reduces the risk of cancer
Lowers the risk of heart disease

Helps prevent type 2 diabetes

## Example 2: Cooking

*Context*
a. Background: The user is looking for a vegetarian pasta recipe.
b. Constraints: The recipe should be simple, use common ingredients, and serve 4 people.
*Task Definition*
a. Objective: Provide a vegetarian pasta recipe.
b. Requirements: Include a list of ingredients, quantities, and step-by-step instructions.
*Examples (optional)*
a. Sample Input: "Can you give me a simple vegetarian pasta recipe?"
b. Sample Output:
*Ingredients:*
12 oz. spaghetti
2 tbsp. olive oil
1 onion, chopped
2 cloves garlic, minced
1 can (28 oz.) crushed tomatoes
1/4 cup fresh basil, chopped
Salt and pepper to taste
Grated Parmesan cheese (optional)
*Instructions:*
Cook spaghetti according to package instructions.
In a large skillet, heat olive oil over medium heat. Add onion and garlic; sauté until softened.
Add crushed tomatoes, salt, and pepper; simmer for 15 minutes.
Stir in fresh basil.
Drain spaghetti and toss with sauce. Serve with Parmesan cheese, if desired.

## Example 3: Time Management

*Context*
a. Background: The user is asking for advice on how to improve their time management skills.
b. Constraints: The response should focus on practical tips and strategies.
*Task Definition*
a. Objective: Provide time management tips and strategies.
b. Requirements: Give at least five actionable tips for improving time management.
Examples (optional)
a. Sample Input: "How can I improve my time management skills?"
b. Sample Output:

Set clear goals and prioritize tasks.
Break tasks into smaller, manageable pieces.
Use a calendar or planner to organize your schedule.
Allocate specific time blocks for focused work.
Eliminate distractions and avoid multitasking.

## Example 4: Book summary

*Context*
a. Background: The user wants a summary of the book "To Kill a Mockingbird" by Harper Lee.
b. Constraints: The summary should be spoiler-free and under 100 words.
*Task Definition*
a. Objective: Provide a brief, spoiler-free summary of "To Kill a Mockingbird."
b. Requirements: The summary should be concise and not exceed 100 words.
*Examples (optional)*
a. Sample Input: "Can you give me a short summary of 'To Kill a Mockingbird'?"
b. Sample Output: "To Kill a Mockingbird" is a novel by Harper Lee that tells the story of Scout Finch and her brother, Jem, growing up in the racially divided town of Maycomb, Alabama during the 1930s. The story explores themes of racial injustice, moral growth, and the importance of empathy through the children's experiences and their father, Atticus Finch, a principled lawyer who defends a black man accused of a crime he didn't commit.

## Example 5: Differences

*Context*
a. Background: The user wants to know the difference between a savings account and a checking account.
b. Constraints: The response should be concise and focus on the key differences between the two.
*Task Definition*
a. Objective: Explain the key differences between a savings account and a checking account.
b. Requirements: Provide a brief comparison, highlighting at least three main differences.
*Examples (optional)*
a. Sample Input: "What is the difference between a savings account and a checking account?"
b. Sample Output:
Savings accounts are designed for long-term savings and typically offer higher interest rates, while checking accounts are meant for everyday transactions and offer lower or no interest.
Checking accounts provide easier access to funds through checks, debit cards, and ATMs, while savings accounts may have withdrawal limits or restrictions.

Savings accounts often have minimum balance requirements or limits on transactions to encourage saving, while checking accounts usually have fewer restrictions on usage.

## Example 6: Listings

*Context*
a. Background: The user wants a list of popular tourist attractions in New York City.
b. Constraints: The response should include at least five major attractions.
*Task Definition*
a. Objective: List popular tourist attractions in New York City.
b. Requirements: Provide a list of at least five major attractions.
*Examples (optional)*
a. Sample Input: "What are some popular tourist attractions in New York City?"
b. Sample Output:
Statue of Liberty
Central Park
Times Square
Empire State Building
Metropolitan Museum of Art

## Example 7: General knowledge

*Context*
a. Background: The user wants to know the benefits of practicing yoga regularly.
b. Constraints: The response should be concise and focus on the health benefits of yoga.
*Task Definition*
a. Objective: Explain the health benefits of regular yoga practice.
b. Requirements: Provide a list of at least five health benefits.
*Examples (optional)*
a. Sample Input: "What are the benefits of practicing yoga regularly?"
b. Sample Output:
Improved flexibility and posture
Increased muscle strength and tone
Enhanced mental clarity and focus
Reduced stress and anxiety
Improved cardiovascular health

## Example 8: Finding Tips

*Context*
a. Background: The user is looking for tips on how to maintain a healthy work-life balance.
b. Constraints: The response should focus on practical advice and include at least five tips.
*Task Definition*

a. Objective: Provide tips on maintaining a healthy work-life balance.
b. Requirements: Give at least five actionable tips.
*Examples (optional)*
a. Sample Input: "How can I maintain a healthy work-life balance?"
b. Sample Output:
Set boundaries between work and personal life.
Prioritize self-care, such as exercise, sleep, and healthy eating.
Learn to delegate tasks and avoid overcommitting.
Schedule regular breaks and downtime.
Cultivate hobbies and interests outside of work.

## Example 9: Information

*Context*
a. Background: The user wants to know the main causes of climate change.
b. Constraints: The response should be concise and focus on the key factors contributing to climate change.
*Task Definition*
a. Objective: Explain the main causes of climate change.
b. Requirements: Provide a brief explanation of at least three key factors.
*Examples (optional)*
a. Sample Input: "What are the main causes of climate change?"
b. Sample Output:
Greenhouse gas emissions from human activities, such as burning fossil fuels for energy, agriculture, and deforestation.
- Deforestation, which reduces the Earth's capacity to absorb carbon dioxide and contributes to greenhouse gas emissions.
- Methane emissions from livestock, agriculture, and the decomposition of organic waste in landfills.

## Example 10: Brief history

*Context*
a. Background: The user wants to know about the history of the internet.
b. Constraints: The response should provide a brief overview of the internet's history, focusing on key milestones.
*Task Definition*
a. Objective: Provide a brief history of the internet.
b. Requirements: Include at least three key milestones in the development of the internet.
*Examples (optional)*
a. Sample Input: "Can you tell me about the history of the internet?"
b. Sample Output:
- The internet traces its origins to the 1960s, when the US Department of Defense developed ARPANET, a network of computers designed to share information and resources.

- In the 1980s, the development of the Transmission Control Protocol (TCP) and the Internet Protocol (IP) allowed for the interconnection of different networks, giving birth to the modern internet.
- The World Wide Web, invented by Tim Berners-Lee in 1989, revolutionized the way people access and share information, transforming the internet into the vast global network we know today.

## Weak versus Strong Prompts

| WEAK PROMPTS | STRONG PROMPTS |
|---|---|
| 1. "Describe the differences between renewable and non-renewable energy sources." | 1. "Given the increasing global concerns about climate change, describe the differences between renewable and non-renewable energy sources, highlighting their environmental impact and long-term sustainability." |
| 2. "Summarize the main events of the French Revolution." | 2. "Considering the historical significance of the French Revolution, summarize its main events, including the causes, key figures, and its influence on modern political systems." |
| 3. "Provide a step-by-step guide on how to bake chocolate chip cookies." | 3. "For a beginner baker interested in making homemade treats, provide a step-by-step guide on how to bake chocolate chip cookies, including the ingredients, measurements, and baking instructions." |
| 4. "Explain the process of photosynthesis in plants." | 4. "To help a high school student understand plant biology, explain the process of photosynthesis in plants, detailing the stages involved and the importance of this process for life on Earth." |
| 5. "Write a short story about a time-traveling adventurer." | 5. "Inspire creativity by writing a short story about a time-traveling adventurer who visits three distinct historical periods, encountering various challenges and making impactful decisions along the way." |
| 6. "Discuss the impact of artificial intelligence on the job market." | 6. "In the context of the ongoing technological revolution, discuss the impact of artificial intelligence on the job market, addressing both potential job losses and the emergence of new job opportunities." |
| 7. "Create a sample itinerary for a 7-day trip to Japan." | 7. "Create a sample itinerary for a 7-day trip to Japan for a first-time visitor, highlighting must-see attractions, local cuisine recommendations, and cultural experiences in Tokyo, Kyoto, and Osaka." |
| 8. "Compare and contrast the economic systems of capitalism and socialism." | 8. "From an economic perspective, compare and contrast the principles and outcomes of capitalism and socialism, examining their strengths, weaknesses, and real-world examples of their implementation." |
| 9. "Suggest five strategies to improve work-life balance." | 9. "To address the challenges of modern work culture, suggest five practical strategies to improve work-life balance, emphasizing mental well-being and long-term productivity." |
| 10. "Analyze the themes of love and jealousy in Shakespeare's Othello." | 10. "Delve into the literary analysis of Shakespeare's Othello by examining the themes of love and jealousy, discussing how they intertwine throughout the play and contribute to the tragic outcome." |

**Samples of ChatGPT Simple Instructions**

- Give me step-by-step instructions for making a smoothie.
- Walk me through the process of creating a budget.
- Break down the steps to changing a flat tire.
- In a step-by-step manner, explain how to knit a scarf.
- Provide a detailed, step-by-step guide for setting up a fish tank.
- Sequentially describe the process of installing a new app on a smartphone.
- Stepwise, how do I meditate for stress relief?
- Can you outline the steps for assembling IKEA furniture?
- What are the steps in order for making a perfect omelette?
- Teach me how to do a simple magic trick.
- Explain the process of writing a cover letter.
- Guide me through the steps of folding an origami crane.
- Show me how to take a screenshot on a computer.
- Provide instructions for making homemade pizza.
- How do I create a strong password?
- Can you help me with troubleshooting Wi-Fi connection issues?
- Describe the method for calculating compound interest.
- What is the procedure to replace a smoke detector battery?
- Demonstrate how to tie a bow tie.
- Give me ideas for planning a surprise birthday party.
- Summarize the main events of World War II.
- Translate the phrase "Hello, how are you?" into Spanish.
- Act as a virtual assistant and help me manage my calendar.
- Let's think step-by-step about creating a workout routine.
- Write in the style of Shakespeare a short love poem.
- Show me how to plant and care for a vegetable garden.
- Provide instructions for cooking a romantic dinner for two.
- How do I create a successful crowdfunding campaign?
- Can you help me with learning basic photography skills?
- Describe the method for building a simple treehouse.

# Prompts for Image Generators

Artificial Intelligence (AI) image generators have revolutionized the field of computer graphics and design, enabling users to create unique and compelling visuals with ease. These advanced tools utilize deep learning algorithms, typically powered by Generative Adversarial Networks (GANs), to synthesize realistic images based on text inputs or prompts. This article will provide an overview of AI image generators and offer guidance on crafting effective prompts to maximize their potential.

## AI Image Generators:

At the heart of AI image generators are GANs, which consist of two neural networks: a generator and a discriminator. The generator creates new images, while the discriminator evaluates their quality and authenticity. As the generator improves its output, the discriminator becomes more discerning, leading to increasingly realistic images.

Popular AI image generators include OpenAI's DALL-E , Midjourney, and NVIDIA's StyleGAN. DALL-E can generate images from natural language descriptions, while StyleGAN is known for creating high-quality portraits, landscapes, and other visual content. Both of these tools, along with others in the field, are continually evolving, providing artists and designers with new possibilities for creative expression.

# Crafting Prompts for AI Image Generators

To harness the full potential of AI image generators, it is essential to provide them with well-crafted prompts. The following guidelines will help users create prompts that result in unique and engaging visuals:

**Clarity and specificity:** Be clear and specific about what you want the AI to generate. Vague prompts may result in unpredictable outcomes. If you have a particular subject, style, or setting in mind, make sure to include those details in your prompt.

**Keep it concise:** While providing specific details is crucial, try to keep your prompts concise. Overly lengthy prompts may confuse the AI or dilute the focus of the generated image.

**Use descriptive language**: AI image generators do not understand grammar or sentence structure in the same way humans do. Instead, they rely on the semantics of the words used in the prompt. Use vivid and descriptive language to convey your vision.

**Focus on desired elements:** Describe the elements you want to include in the image rather than those you want to exclude. AI image generators might still include unwanted elements if the prompt mentions them, even in a negative context.

**Experiment with variations:** Sometimes, rephrasing a prompt or changing the order of words can yield different results. Don't hesitate to experiment with various prompt structures and phrasings to achieve the desired output.

**Incorporate image URLs (when applicable):** Some AI image generators allow users to include image URLs in their prompts. These URLs can influence the style and content of the generated image, providing additional creative control.

**Utilize parameters:** Many AI image generators offer parameters that users can adjust to influence the final output. These parameters can include aspect ratios, models, upscalers, and more. Experiment with different parameters to achieve the desired effect.

**Iterate and refine:** It's not uncommon for AI image generators to produce unexpected results. If the generated image doesn't meet your expectations, revise your prompt and try again. Iteration and refinement are key to obtaining the perfect image.

**AI image generation models**

There are several AI image generation models available, each with unique characteristics and training approaches. Some of the most popular ones include:

- **GANs (Generative Adversarial Networks):** GANs consist of two neural networks, a generator and a discriminator, that compete against each other in a zero-sum game. The generator creates realistic images while the discriminator tries to distinguish between real and generated images. GANs have been used for various image generation tasks, including image synthesis, style transfer, and image-to-image translation.

- **VAEs (Variational Autoencoders):** VAEs are a type of generative model that learns the latent representation of the input data. They consist of an encoder and a decoder. The encoder compresses the input into a latent space, while the decoder reconstructs the original input from the latent representation. VAEs have been used for image synthesis, interpolation, and denoising.

- **DALLE-2 (Deep Abstract Latent Language Exposition 2):** Developed by OpenAI, DALLE-2 is a model that generates images from textual descriptions. It is trained using a combination of unsupervised and supervised learning, with a focus on aligning the generated images with the input text prompts.

- **CLIP (Contrastive Language-Image Pretraining):** Another model from OpenAI, CLIP is trained on a large dataset of images and text pairs. It learns to generate images by optimizing for similarity between the image and text embeddings. CLIP has been used for zero-shot image classification, image synthesis, and image-captioning tasks.

- **StyleGAN (Style Generative Adversarial Network):** StyleGAN is an advanced GAN architecture introduced by NVIDIA that generates high-quality images. It uses adaptive instance normalization (AdaIN) and a progressive growing training scheme to create realistic images. StyleGAN has been used for tasks like face synthesis, art generation, and style transfer.

- **BigGAN (Big Generative Adversarial Network):** BigGAN is a GAN architecture designed to generate high-resolution images by scaling up the model size and training on large-scale datasets. It introduces techniques like self-attention and spectral normalization to improve the quality of generated images.

These models have been trained on large datasets containing millions of images, such as ImageNet, CelebA, and COCO, as well as domain-specific datasets for tasks like art or medical imaging. The models are typically trained using a combination of supervised and unsupervised learning techniques, depending on their architecture and purpose. The primary difference between these models lies in their architecture, training data, and the specific techniques used to generate and refine the images.

**Example of Image Generator Prompts**

- A smiling 13-year-old brunette girl is engrossed in studying books in her stylish bedroom, adorned with cool jewel-toned colors, ambient lighting, and trendy decor. The room's atmosphere reflects her vibrant personality, with niji and upbeta elements integrated into the design.

- An intricately detailed 4k and 8k children's book illustration presents a full-bodied African girl in an anime style. She sports a friendly face, short straight hair, and exudes an air of luxury, as if she's a millionaire. The image boasts rich, vivid colors and a meticulously crafted digital art aesthetic in high-definition.

- A mesmerizing, hyper-realistic photograph captures a glamorous femme fatale woman in a fashion editorial style. She's sitting on a luxurious leather sofa, clad in a low-cut, curve-hugging dress that reveals her décolletage. Her dynamic pose and the professional post-processing, coupled with cinematic studio lighting, create a visually stunning image with intricate details and depth of field.

- A visually captivating portrait features a 25-year-old woman with flowing long hair, perfect, flawless skin, and striking facial features. Her confident three-quarter gaze exudes allure and poise. She's surrounded by a serene, tranquil setting with soft, warm light emanating from a sunbeam. The ultra-high-resolution, 8K image showcases her entire body, highlighting her slender thighs, charming smile, and other alluring aspects in a professional, high-quality fashion photograph.

- A delightful black-and-white coloring page depicts a joyful girl sitting comfortably, engrossed in writing in her diary. The image offers high clarity and bold lines that emphasize her smile and the contours of her figure, making it ideal for coloring enthusiasts of all ages.

- A visually striking abstract landscape artwork features two African women dancing with exuberance amidst a high-contrast setting inspired by a jazz festival. The piece, reminiscent of Van Gogh's distinctive style, showcases bold brushstrokes, vibrant colors, and dynamic movement, effortlessly blending the energy of dance and music into a captivating visual experience.

AI image generators have opened up a new world of possibilities for artists, designers, and content creators. By understanding how these powerful tools work and following the guidelines for crafting effective prompts, users can unlock their full potential and create stunning visuals that were once unimaginable. As AI technology continues to advance, the possibilities for creative expression through AI image generators will only expand, ushering in a new era of art and design.

# Reference

BigGAN (Big Generative Adversarial Network): Brock, A., Donahue, J., & Simonyan, K. (2018). Large scale GAN training for high fidelity natural image synthesis. arXiv preprint arXiv:1809.11096. https://arxiv.org/abs/1809.11096

CLIP (Contrastive Language-Image Pretraining): Radford, A., Kim, J. W., Hallacy, C., Ramesh, A., Goh, G., Agarwal, S., ... & Sutskever, I. (2021). Learning Transferable Visual Models From Natural Language Supervision. arXiv preprint arXiv:2103.00020. https://arxiv.org/abs/2103.00020

DALLE-2 (Deep Abstract Latent Language Exposition 2): OpenAI has not yet published a paper on DALLE-2, but you can find more information on their blog post: https://openai.com/research/dall-e-2/

GANs (Generative Adversarial Networks): Goodfellow, I., Pouget-Abadie, J., Mirza, M., Xu, B., Warde-Farley, D., Ozair, S., ... & Bengio, Y. (2014). Generative adversarial nets. Advances in neural information processing systems, 27, 2672-2680. https://arxiv.org/abs/1406.2661

StyleGAN (Style Generative Adversarial Network): Karras, T., Laine, S., & Aila, T. (2018). A style-based generator architecture for generative adversarial networks. In Proceedings of the IEEE/CVF Conference on Computer Vision and Pattern Recognition (pp. 4401-4410). https://arxiv.org/abs/1812.04948

VAEs (Variational Autoencoders): Kingma, D. P., & Welling, M. (2013). Auto-encoding variational bayes. arXiv preprint arXiv:1312.6114. https://arxiv.org/abs/1312.6114

# NOTE #13

## Legal and Ethical Considerations

Legal, ethical, and copyright considerations surrounding AI-generated images can be complex and are often subject to ongoing debates and evolving legal frameworks. In general, the ownership and rights of AI-generated images can depend on various factors, such as the jurisdiction, the specific AI system, the input data, and the involvement of human creators. Here are some general points to consider:

Copyright ownership: In many jurisdictions, copyright law requires a human creator for a work to be eligible for protection. As a result, AI-generated images may not qualify for copyright protection if there is no human authorship involved. However, this can vary depending on the jurisdiction and the degree of human intervention.

- **Rights to input data:** The rights to AI-generated images can also depend on the rights to the input data used to train the AI system. If the training data includes copyrighted materials, the generated images may infringe on the copyrights of the original authors, unless the use of such data falls under exceptions like fair use or other legal provisions.

- **AI system developers and users:** Developers of AI systems and those who use the systems to generate images may have contractual agreements that outline the ownership and usage rights of the generated images. For example, some AI platforms may require users to grant specific licenses to the platform or may claim ownership of the generated images.

- **Ethical considerations:** The use of AI-generated images can raise ethical concerns, such as privacy, consent, and manipulation. For example, generating images of real people without their consent or creating deepfake images to deceive others can lead to ethical and legal issues.

- **Evolving legal frameworks:** Legal frameworks surrounding AI-generated content are evolving, and lawmakers in different jurisdictions may enact new laws or update existing ones to address the unique challenges posed by AI-generated images.

Given the complex nature of these issues, it is essential to stay informed about the legal and ethical considerations in the jurisdiction where the AI-generated images are created and used. Consulting with legal professionals can help ensure compliance with relevant laws and ethical guidelines.

# Conclusion

Prompt engineering is a crucial aspect of natural language processing (NLP) systems that holds the potential to revolutionize how we interact with these systems. In this book, we delved into the core aspects of prompt engineering, covering its definition, significance, and applications. We also examined techniques for effective prompt engineering, such as data collection and preparation, exploratory data analysis, and the selection and crafting of prompts. Lastly, we investigated the future of prompt engineering, encompassing emerging technologies, ethical considerations, as well as challenges and opportunities.

As a rapidly evolving field, prompt engineering has the capacity to reshape our engagement with NLP systems. With advancements in AI and machine learning, prompt engineering is becoming increasingly sophisticated, enabling the generation of more accurate and contextually relevant responses. As this field continues to develop, it is essential to consider the ethical ramifications of its applications and address the challenges and opportunities that emerge. Through meticulous planning and execution, prompt engineering can enhance the accuracy and relevance of NLP systems, significantly impacting various industries and domains.

# Summary of Key Takeaways

From this book (I still would have preferred calling a notes) , we (human and robots) can summarize some key takeaways about prompt engineering:

- Prompt engineering is the process of designing and refining prompts to improve the quality and relevance of the generated responses from NLP systems.

- Effective prompt engineering requires careful consideration and attention to detail, including data collection and preparation, exploratory data analysis, and selecting and crafting prompts.

- Prompt engineering has a wide range of practical applications, including chatbots and virtual assistants, customer service automation, content creation, and fraud detection.

- Emerging technologies in AI and machine learning, such as GPT-3, few-shot learning, and reinforcement learning, are likely to have a significant impact on prompt engineering.

- Ethical considerations in prompt engineering, such as bias, privacy, and transparency, must be carefully considered to ensure that NLP systems are used ethically and responsibly.

Final Thoughts and Recommendations

Prompt engineering is an exciting and rapidly evolving field with the potential to transform the way we interact with NLP systems. To achieve the full potential of prompt engineering, it is important to approach it with a careful and thoughtful mindset, considering the ethical implications of its use and addressing the challenges and opportunities that arise.

As a recommendation, it is important to stay up to date with the latest developments in prompt engineering and emerging technologies in AI and machine learning. It is also important to consider the ethical implications of prompt engineering and ensure that NLP systems are used ethically and responsibly. Finally, we recommend investing in training and education in prompt engineering to develop the necessary skills and knowledge to design and refine prompts effectively.

In conclusion, prompt engineering is a critical component of NLP systems that has the potential to transform the way we interact with these systems. The fundamentals of prompt engineering include its definition, importance, and applications. Techniques for effective prompt engineering include data collection and preparation, exploratory data analysis, selecting and crafting prompts, and evaluation metrics. The future of prompt engineering is closely tied to emerging technologies in AI and machine learning, ethical considerations, and challenges and opportunities.

As prompt engineering continues to evolve, it is important to approach it with a careful and thoughtful mindset. We must consider the ethical implications of its use and address the challenges and opportunities that arise. By investing in training and education in prompt engineering and staying up to date with the latest developments in the field, we can ensure that NLP systems are used ethically and responsibly and achieve the full potential of prompt engineering.

"Mastering Prompt Engineering: A Comprehensive Guide for Beginners"

Natural language processing (NLP) is a rapidly evolving field with a wide range of practical applications. At the heart of any successful NLP system is prompt engineering, which involves designing and refining prompts to improve the accuracy and relevance of the generated responses. "Mastering Prompt Engineering: A Comprehensive Guide for Beginners" is a practical and comprehensive guide to prompt engineering, from the fundamentals to the latest advances and emerging technologies.

# Glossary of Term Related to AI, Natural Language Processing, and Prompt Engineering

Active Learning: A machine learning technique where a model actively queries a human expert for labels during the training process, typically focusing on the most uncertain or informative examples.

AI (Artificial Intelligence): The development of computer systems that can perform tasks typically requiring human intelligence, such as visual perception, speech recognition, decision-making, and natural language understanding.

Attention Mechanism: A technique used in neural networks, particularly transformers, to weigh the importance of different input elements when generating an output.

Autoencoder: A type of neural network used for unsupervised learning, which learns to compress input data into a lower-dimensional representation and then reconstruct the original data from that representation.

BERT (Bidirectional Encoder Representations from Transformers): A transformer-based model developed by Google that uses bidirectional training to better understand the context of words in a sentence.

Bias: Systematic errors in an AI model's predictions, often resulting from limitations or imbalances in the training data.

Chatbot: An AI-powered conversational agent that interacts with users via text or voice, simulating human-like conversation.

Data Augmentation: The process of generating new training examples from existing data to improve the performance and generalization of AI models.

Deep Learning: A subset of machine learning that uses artificial neural networks to model complex patterns and representations in large datasets, enabling advanced capabilities such as image and speech recognition.

Evaluation Metrics: Quantitative measures used to assess the performance of AI models, such as accuracy, precision, recall, F1 score, and perplexity.

Explainable AI (XAI): An area of AI research focused on developing techniques and methods to make AI models more transparent, understandable, and interpretable for human users.

Fine-tuning: The process of adjusting a pre-trained AI model's weights and parameters to adapt it to a specific task or domain.

GAN (Generative Adversarial Network): A type of deep learning model consisting of two neural networks, a generator and a discriminator, which work together to generate realistic samples from training data.

GPT (Generative Pre-trained Transformer): A family of large-scale transformer-based language models developed by OpenAI, known for their ability to generate coherent and contextually relevant text.

Human-in-the-Loop: An approach to AI system development that involves human intervention or collaboration, often to validate or refine the system's outputs or to provide additional training data

Levenshtein Distance: A metric for measuring the similarity between two strings by calculating the minimum number of single-character edits (insertions, deletions, or substitutions) required to transform one string into the other.

Machine Learning: A subset of AI that involves the development of algorithms that enable systems to learn from data and improve their performance over time without explicit programming.

Machine Translation: The automatic translation of text from one language to another using AI and NLP techniques.

Named Entity Recognition (NER): The process of identifying and classifying named entities (e.g., people, organizations, locations) within a text.

Neural Networks: Computational models inspired by the structure and function of the human brain, used to recognize patterns, make predictions, and process data in AI systems.

NLP (Natural Language Processing): The area of AI focused on enabling machines to understand, interpret, generate, and interact with human language.

Parsing: The analysis of text to determine its grammatical structure and the relationships between words or phrases.

POS (Part-of-Speech) Tagging: The process of assigning grammatical categories (e.g., noun, verb, adjective) to tokens in a text.

Prompt Engineering: The process of designing and refining input prompts to elicit desired outputs from AI language models, enhancing their performance and usability.

Question Answering: A task in NLP that involves generating a response to a given question based on a provided context, such as a passage of text or a knowledge base.

Reinforcement Learning: A type of machine learning where an agent learns to make decisions by interacting with its environment and receiving feedback in the form of rewards or penalties.

Sentiment Analysis: The use of NLP techniques to determine the emotional tone or attitude expressed in a piece of text.

Seq2Seq (Sequence-to-Sequence) Model: A type of neural network architecture designed for tasks that involve mapping one sequence to another, such as machine translation or text summarization.

Supervised Learning: A type of machine learning where a model is trained using labeled data, with input-output pairs provided to learn the underlying pattern or relationship.

Text Classification: The task of assigning predefined categories or labels to a given text based on its content.

Text Summarization: The process of creating a concise representation of a larger document or set of documents, preserving only the most important information.

Tokenization: The process of breaking text into individual words or tokens for further analysis in NLP.

Topic Modeling: An unsupervised learning technique used to discover abstract topics or themes within a collection of documents.

Transfer Learning: A technique in machine learning where a model trained on one task is adapted to perform a different, but related, task with minimal additional training.

Transformer: A deep learning architecture introduced by Vaswani et al. (2017), known for its self-attention mechanism, which allows it to efficiently process long-range dependencies in sequences.

Turing Test: A test proposed by Alan Turing to assess a machine's ability to exhibit intelligent behavior indistinguishable from that of a human.

Unsupervised Learning: A type of machine learning where a model is trained using unlabeled data, with the goal of discovering hidden structures or patterns within the data.

Word Embeddings: Vector representations of words that capture their semantic meaning and relationships, commonly used as input for NLP models.

**"Mastering Prompt Engineering: A Comprehensive Guide for Beginners."**

Dive into the fascinating world of natural language processing with "Mastering Prompt Engineering: A Comprehensive Guide for Beginners." This one-of-a-kind resource, written by a team of robots and a novice human learner, provides an engaging and accessible introduction to the latest advances in prompt engineering. Immerse yourself in the book's unique structure, which covers everything from the fundamentals to practical applications, and even offers a glimpse into the future of this exciting field. As you navigate through the chapters, you'll discover the book's extensive coverage of key topics, making it an essential addition to any NLP library.

Unlock the potential of prompt engineering and transform the way you interact with AI systems. With "Mastering Prompt Engineering," you'll gain invaluable insights into effective techniques, innovative applications, and the future of this rapidly evolving field. Whether you're a student, researcher, or practitioner in NLP, this comprehensive guide is the perfect resource to fuel your passion and drive your success in the world of prompt engineering. Don't miss out on this opportunity to explore the fascinating realm of NLP—get your copy today and start your journey towards mastering prompt engineering!

www.ingramcontent.com/pod-product-compliance
Lightning Source LLC
Chambersburg PA
CBHW080521060326
40690CB00038B/5210